(CLOSE)
DAVID MILLER

Newton-le-Willows

Published in the United Kingdom in 2023
by The Knives Forks And Spoons Press,
51 Pipit Avenue,
Newton-le-Willows,
Merseyside,
WA12 9RG.

ISBN 978-1-912211-96-8

Copyright © David Miller 2023.

The right of David Miller to be identified as the author of this work has been asserted by them in accordance with the Copyrights, Designs and Patents Act of 1988. All rights reserved. No part of this publication may be reproduced, stored in a retrieval system, transmitted in any form or by any means, electronic, photocopying, recording or otherwise, without prior permission of the publisher.

Cover image: *Ink Painting (D&D)* by David Miler © 2023

Acknowledgements:

Some of these pieces have appeared in *International Times (IT)*, *Kater Murr's Press*, *Oasis*, *Osiris*, *otata's bookshelf*, *otoliths*, *Shearsman*, *Stride* and *Tears in the Fence*.

A few of them also appeared in *Some Other Days and Nights*, a pamphlet from above/ground press in Canada, 2021. Many thanks to rob mclennan.

The first two variations of *suddenness* appeared in A *River Flowing Beside*, SF: hawkhaven press, 2013. Many thanks to Wiliam Cirocco.

The Dark Path: An earlier version of this piece appeared in *Five Fingers Review* #17, Berkeley, 1998. This version was originally published as a booklet by tel-let (Charleston, IL) in 2000, in an edition of 75 copies. Many thanks to John Martone. It has since appeared online on the *Creative Critical* website (https://creativecritical.net/the-dark-path/).

Contents

(close)   5

(a step out)   17

(an indoors idyll)   25

(hares)   29

(for a death)   35

(things unhidden since the beginning)   39

(the dance)   45

(six poems)   51

(suddenness)   61

(the day Valerie Solanas shot Andy Warhol)   69

(the dark path)   75

(notes)   89

(close)

1.

full light half-light near-light near-dark half-dark full dark

red yellow blue close to dark close to light

close

    * * *

who's afraid? I

I am

or
unsettled

going into
going out

(uncanonical)

tears
elsewhere

David Miller

2.

there were black lines
& white spaces

but before that
a grey tree

& the sea spread out before us
the sea? scar on my arm & the sea

spread out before us
black lines & white spaces

    * * *

to dance

to dance yes

& the sea

before us

grey

    * * *

gotta dance

I didn't
I never did

though I was asked

3.

weeping

black
white

    * * *

forsaken
or so he thought

in pain

in pain
forsaken

    * * *

yet cleaving to

4.

tears
in canvas

tears
in fabric

tears?
not in canvas

or in fabric

tears
just the same

      * * *

scared yes

yes sometimes
sometimes indeed afraid

or scarred

or seared

(the Sublime)

I would fly away & be at rest

at rest
in the sacred

5.

not peace
but a sword

not a sword
but peace

I have come to bring division
to separate

& yet
how blest are the peacemakers

    * * *

cleaved to
cleaving to

6.

black sky
black sea

black

so I've heard
so I've read

so I've seen

7.

breath
her breath

a breath
no breath

face pared down
ah everything pared down

& yet elongated

& paused
or poised

her eyes
so kind

kindness
yes

passed
she was

breath stops

& is

breath-
lessly

    * * *

for a widower
nothing is won

except his wife's release

David Miller

8.

aesthetics
inadequate

he said

to what?
even

he said
to itself

    * * *

how needful it is to enter into the darkness
& to admit the coincidence of opposites

to seek where impossibility meets us

9.

death is not an event in life
– dying is

though un-
original

to say

if
also

un-
trivially

lacking

    * * *

to cleave
to be close

close

how needful
where impossibility meets us

(in memory of Dodo)

(a step out)

the bear cub
looks back

in fright

small bear
the hunt is on

escape?
but how?

the orphaned
koala joey

clutches
a human arm

eyes
eyes that look that search that beseech

the small bear
also seeking comfort

eyes speaking
of trauma

or medicine
the little bear?

needs sleep
& dream

after escape
yes dream

dream play

dream vision
ah spirit vision

stone leaves

David Miller

& rain
& flood

we wanted to help him
yes but how?

  * * *

the stone lion
the eucalyptus tree

the birds
as always

drinking ... so?
so meditatively

from the stone
ceramic or metal

drinking vessels

the studio door
open

that I might paint or draw

  * * *

the monkey puzzle
died

the eucalyptus
thrives

  * * *

the windows
in need of repair

so get out on the ledge
to patch them up

with whatever you find
to repair

hold in place
for a while

    * * *

the windows
come unstuck

fallen apart
ah yes

de-
structured

the view
no view

we saw a frame
we saw through it

but the frame
came undone

doubled first
then dissolved

    * * *

David Miller

central London
's

in ruins

not from bombings
or any battles

implosion
perhaps

& there are strange back streets
with strange shops

& late night clubs
& cafés & bars

so strange

I lived there so long
I won't return

    * * *

bread cheese & butter
red kidney beans & rice

eggs with salad

the lamp burns
the window burns

the door key
shines in the night

& a meal is not a meal
not simply so

the window
the blue house

if the dark is illimitable
there is no window

there is a sea
a dark sea a black sea utterly black

   * * *

a light goes on
a light goes off

a light goes on
with plants in readiness

palms & orchids
roses & gardenias

they're waiting ah yes
waiting in radiance

& your dance awaits
your green sparkly hat

green lipstick
for effect

a walking stick of course
with faux-marble handle

   * * *

a step away
a step towards

David Miller

no

lying on the bed
so thin

so fragile
yes

    * * *

that long slow walk
in the night

which we could track
so slowly & gracefully

so poignantly

but is it ever more
than a step a step

away yes a step away?
that she takes

(in memory of Dodo)

(an indoors idyll)

wind

rain sleet snow
mist

fog

    * * *

to drink:
advocaat

or white
or red wine

to eat:
aubergines

spring greens
dill & spring onions

&
avocado

with pepper salt
& extra

virgin olive oil

    * * *

shared

(hares)

hare coursing

if I had to
no

a harvest mouse

drinking milk
from a jug

front paws
on the lip

yellow
& then hares

if I had to

* * *

if I had to
but no

no necessity

blood
of course

& some do

over fields
out of veins

through veins
over fields

* * *

David Miller

there was a blind cat
called Homer

& a cat whose eyes
etched the word "fish"

into the window glass

"I didn't come to this holy island
to castrate stray cats!"

seldom angry
a rare occasion

a rare person
a rare poet

as it happened

    * * *

know or not
know

learn
to not know

wisteria
or oranges on the vine

dear (dead) friends
I address

not just one

    * * *

& not only one

candle flame
no

not yet
while fires persist

burning
though rain falls

    * * *

unknowing

unknowing?
yes

    * * *

hare coursing
negated

in an afterlife

and now?

(in memory of Robert Lax)

(for a death)

don't say a word   look
at the oriented
grass in thick clumps
combed driven

polished bronze
reflected water
a man stops
in death his body
green through the
taut cloth
holding him
slumped suspended

those poor
hands cupped
around aurum

*(things unhidden
since
the beginning)*

scars
&

the perfect

the perfect

&
scars

    * * *

the scars of martyrdom

some want to see
persecution anyway

or the scars of accident
& mental illness

    * * *

milk curds
shared

(martyrdom)

    * * *

ah but not
the beginning no

David Miller

where is your brother?
his blood is crying out

from the ground
whose mouth

has opened wide

  * * *

ah but to kill
oneself

or others
or to maim

oneself
or others

I can't see
I can't

I can't
I can't

I can

  * * *

the buildings
labyrinthine

their passages
& stories

even the steps
outside

where I lost
all I owned

    * * *

& before
& after

(the dance)

dance even
to gospel

yes
dance

but not
to Gregorian chant

yet Christ danced
a round dance

(or so
St John)

    * * *

a lamp am I
a mirror am I

a door am I
a way am I

I would be saved
& I would save

I would be loosed
& I would loose

I would be wounded
& I would wound

I would be washed
& I would wash

I would eat
& I would be eaten

    * * *

David Miller

(if
apocryphal

then
apocryphal)

(to the memory of Sydney Carter)

(six poems)

Portrait from a Dream

We hadn't seen each other for a long time, when he buttonholed me in the street, talking in a way aimed to embarrass; but what most disturbed me was how much illness had changed his appearance. He followed me back to the small, spartan room where I was staying – and suddenly became friendlier, kinder, even inviting me to spend Christmas and New Year with him.
Reversed. He arrived with two suitcases; but stayed only a few days.
'Ironists should die and be buried with their fake leather boots on.'
At the end he spoke somewhat sadly, disappointedly. Rather than fiercely.
On the grass: ice in small circular sheets from the bird baths, broken or entire.

David Miller

    in glass
    glass
    this page
    following
    water a
    broken
    pencil a
    shattered
    mirror
    ……
    here
    there
    translated
    or the same
    your body
    to your body
    you
    to you

From a Sentence of D T Suzuki's

Alizarin yellow. Birds flying in swirls. Cries.
'This spoon *now* exists in Paradise', he exclaimed, holding up a spoon and waving it around.
Another said: *'I drink a glass of water; I die; I drink from a pool of water'*.
My hand, palm up: illuminated.

David Miller

ENCOUNTER

We all sat on the floor; some had disrobed; some took turns playing music on exotic instruments, plucking, bowing, beating, blowing. None of it was moving or stirred me: I became bored, and I was about to get up and leave; but you said first, 'Let's go', pulling a coat around your naked body and buttoning it. When we came to the door and had opened it, we had to leap down. Mud. Silence.

                was it you or an image
                of you *your light*
                a copied light?

                you or a copy
                of you your light
                a copied light

Psychomachia.

"this constant *transference over there*
and *back here* in one act" "One
must remember that the movement
of the senses is toward their proper
objects of love" sky pale blue the buildings
a rag floating a rag gold-crimson a ring
one hand two hands slender and a face
the person begins to be defined
in the darkness of the house a rag
gold-crimson a ring gold-crimson

David Miller

Through corridors,
rectangles, of stone
& sunlight: some-
one moving,
            making

Love's summed
in that which
from repose comes
to an action –
(say) water flowing
to a wound,
           hands

bathing the wound;
or honey flowing
to the mouth which
meets it

(suddenness)

suddenness   transverse

David Miller

								suddenness

								transverse

suddenness

suddenness   transverse

transverse

David Miller

suddenness

transverse   suddenness

transverse

(the day Valerie Solanas shot Andy Warhol)

Close

I was in the process of putting together my second New York show when I heard that Valerie Solanas had shot Andy Warhol.

"Process" is a word I like, but almost no one seems to understand it in relation to my painting.

I don't especially like Andy Warhol, though I was sorry someone had shot him.

Actually, I have to admit that I don't really know Warhol; I've bumped into him at gallery openings, however. And I once went to Max's Kansas City, where he and his entourage hung out. He was there. They were there.

"Joel Loehy?" someone asked. "Right?"

"Yes," I said.

"I missed your last show, but I heard it was really cool!"

Cool! Oh dear.

"I'll have a new one in a few weeks."

"Cool! I'll try to make it."

"Thanks."

He wouldn't. Whoever he was.

So, as I say, I've never really known Warhol. What I don't like is the whole scene around him, the vainglorious hangers-on, mostly talentless, of course. And I don't like his influence.

It seems like a version of the Great American Dream, but with silver helium balloons and the hip, addicted and lost in its wake.

I don't even like his art.

A democratic art? No, an art that's primarily for the snide elite. An innovative art? Only when the stereotypical takes on its appearance – its disguise – and wins, big time. Yes, a mass following in the end. That's the only end worth considering.

Can we see that certain forms of impoverished art have to be called *great* by art critics so that the art can be sold to the museum curators and to collectors, who then also call it great so that they can justify buying it? Why is it supposedly great? The artist is a celebrity; the artwork is a by-product of celebrity status. But how did the artist become a celebrity? Because his (or her) artwork is great. And how did that become the case? Because the artist had become a celebrity. Why did the critics say it was great in the first place? Can I please stop repeating myself? Are you confused enough as it is?

Or do I have to mention the ever present, ever renewed insistence amongst art gallery owners, critics and curators for novelty, for *the next thing*, especially the *glamorous* thing, coupled with the demands of the art market for sales? (Alongside the perennials of the art market, such as poor van Gogh, who sold few paintings in his lifetime.) Even if certain artists seem to step away from those demands (not always very far, and most certainly not someone like Warhol).

I have had exhibitions, as I've said. But I don't really fit the bill. So I suppose what little reputation I have will eventually peter out. As will my shows: galleries will drop me or refuse to take me on. I'm resigned.

By the way, I always insist that in the catalogues for my exhibitions, the paintings don't have titles. They're listed as Painting #1, Painting #2, and so on.

David Miller

When I tell people that Giotto, Duccio and Piero della Francesca are the painters nearest to my own art, they don't seem to make any connection, and of course ask about more modern artists, and I then mention Malevich, Mondrian, Georges Vantongerloo, Ad Reinhardt, Mathias Goeritz … And they look befuddled, more often than not.

They can't see that there are any resemblances. (And some of them nod absently when I mention Vantongerloo or Goeritz.)

Of course there *aren't* any resemblances, not pictorially, at least. My paintings don't really resemble any others.

They don't resemble anything.

They're invisible. Utterly invisible.

You can't see a thing. Because there isn't any thing.

(the dark path)

I.

Begin with

> *verisimilitude –*

with an art of interpretation and possibility, or of "hypothetical situations"

> (the painters Boyd & Evans, in conversation)

"Like" images   *("unlike" images)*

> *Exploration of possibilities –*
> > MULTIPLICITY
> > > (lack of finality or closure)
> > > > Oriole said to Fox: "Oh, come along and let's play. You study too much; it will hurt your back. Why do you ask all those questions from the grown-ups? They don't know the answers. You only embarrass them."
> > > > "But I want to know the truth."
> > > > "What for?"
> > > > "Because I want to know the way it really happened."
> > > > "IT HAPPENED THE WAY they tell it."
> > > > "But they tell it differently!"
> > > > "Then it is because it happened differently."
> > > > (…)
> > > > "All right then," said Tsimmu [the wolf], "I'll tell you the creation story – at least, one of them, because, I tell you, I have heard many different ways of telling it."
> > > > (Jaime de Angulo, *Indian Tales*.)

If *like* images serve an authentic purpose, so do *unlike* images.

> … if anyone condemns these representations as incongruous, suggesting that it is disgraceful to fashion such base images of the divine and most holy Orders [that is, angels], it is sufficient to answer that the most holy Mysteries are set forth in two modes: one, by means of similar and sacred representations akin to their nature, and the other through unlike forms designed with every possible discordance and difference.

David Miller

Moreover:

> If ... the negations in the descriptions of the Divine are true, and the affirmations are inconsistent with It, the exposition of the hidden Mysteries by the use of unlike symbols accords more closely with That which is ineffable.
> (Dionysius the Areopagite, *The Celestial Hierarchies*.)

Like and *unlike*:   *affirmative* and *negative*

    (in a correspondence that admits its own dissonances, irregularities)

        : cataphatic / apophatic (affirmative / negative) theology

Or again: *image / imagelessness*

BUT: Dionysius stresses that the Divine is

    beyond all positive and negative distinctions,

and that

> there is no contradiction between the affirmations and the negations.
> (*The Mystical Theology*.)

Like and unlike images, image and imagelessness –

different ways of disclosing, making-manifest ...

yet there is no contradiction between them.

Dark (black) – light (white)

> Both [white and black] are achromatic and extremes of brightness, and in these respects are interchangeable as symbols, if what has to be symbolized is an extreme state.
>
> (Meyer Schapiro, *Words and Pictures: On the Literal and the Symbolic in the Illustration of a Text*.)

((Again, no contradiction.))

II.

The Negative, the Nameless:

> *What exists is named specifically, and there is no specific name for G-d.*
> (Fanny Howe, *Saving History*.)

> IT, if nameable, is not eternal. The name, nameable, is not eternal name. The Nameless is the root of Heaven and Earth …
> (…)
> To perceive nonperception is the real McCoy.
> (Edwin Denby translating Lao Tzu, *Edwin's Tao*.)

<u>But keeping to the notion of a polarity:</u>

Negative (apophatic) theology

is that everything one thinks of as God – the good, the true, the beautiful, the perfect, the vision of light, all that stuff, he is not those things. He is unknowable, incomprehensible, and finally – one finally has union with that which one cannot know. It is silent, unimagined, unspoken and so on. It is an ecstasy, and there are beautiful ecstasies in Dionysius, but the discipline of it is – and this fascinates me, I think, more than anything else – the discipline is its sensitivity to the language. The moment that one has drawn into the language – and language is basically image before it happens to be syntactical structure and logical movement or any of the rest of our wilfulness, that whole business – all those things God is not. If you say you have seen him and he was dressed in a white robe and he shone magnificently or he's big daddy in the sky with a beard, and think of Blake's Nobodaddy – this is part of Blake's point, that whatever he is he is not. Because you immediately work with a negation of what you know so as not to limit. And there is a tension: I call it experiential dialectic, ultimate polarity, something like this. Now that would be Dionysius the Areopagite's preferred way.
(Robin Blaser, *The Metaphysics of Light*.)

David Miller

One works with affirmation and with negation.

Image/light/affirmation – the metaphysics of light tradition

(from Neoplatonism through Scholasticism and

subsequent Christian intellectual and spiritual traditions) –

an equivalence between ontology (being) and luminosity, so that

> One way or another, the whole of reality turns out, upon examination, to be light in various disguises …
> (Joseph Anthony Mazzeo, *Medieval Cultural Tradition in Dante's 'Comedy'*.)

> It was my hand that wrote me:
> *Pull the covers over your story and say*
> *light, light again and again.*
>
> *Illuminate your pages this way.*
> Fanny Howe, "4:58," *O'Clock*.)

Illumination –

bringing-to-light, disclosing

but also *epiphany*

By epiphany, I mean the apprehension of some spiritual (invisible, immaterial, extra-mundane) dimension, through attention to the particulars of the visible world.

> (Or: what the Canadian realist painter Jack Chambers once referred to as
>
> that faculty of inner vision where the object appears in the splendor of its essential namelessness.
> (Quoted by Nancy Poole, Introduction to *Jack Chambers: Selection of Paintings and Drawings*.)

> Everything and anything that one sees is in its actual presence more than we can in any way understand it to be.
> (Chambers, *Letter to Simon*.))

Here we can mention Grassi's marvellous gloss on Dionysius,

> that divine Beauty is different in every particular being even though in every case we are concerned with the same divine Being. Hence, he [i.e. God] is revealed in every being and yet always hidden in them.
> (Ernesto Grassi, *Heidegger and the Question of Renaissance Humanism*.)

> I could taste the salt of Our Lord's sweat on my tongue at dawn, when there was an orange stripe across the back of the sky.
> (Fanny Howe, *The Lives of a Spirit*.)

Origin:

The question of *origin* appears with our awareness of the Nameless.

> The metaphysics of light tradition is difficult for us to understand because it is an ontology. Ontology is, quite frankly, a language and experience of the beginning, of origin.
> (Robin Blaser, *The Metaphysics of Light*.)

Transposed to a mythological level, we have narratives of origin – but origin is always "other," disclosed but not *contained* by what can be said / shown. ((See Jaime de Angulo's *Indian Tales*, where the time of the main narrative is itself that of "old-time stories," that is, anterior to *our* time; but within that narrative, the characters tell of a time that is prior to their own. The sense of an origin/original time is pushed further and further back.))

III.

> To know anything new is to know it as known.
> (Fanny Howe, "February Three," *O'Clock*.)

> You know by writing that what you know, writes.
> (Fanny Howe, *The Quietist*.)

Or what you *don't* know.

KNOWING / UNKNOWING

Keats' *negative capability*:

> ... I mean *Negative Capability*, that is when man is capable of being in uncertainties, Mysteries, doubts, without any irritable reaching after fact & reason – Coleridge, for instance, would let go by a fine isolated verisimilitude caught from the Penetralium of mystery, from being incapable of remaining content with half knowledge.
> (John Keats, *Letters*.)

Keats' negative capability and the mystical tradition of apophatic theology parallel one another in their emphasis on uncertainty (understood in terms of a negation of *rational certitude*). In both cases, one proceeds by way of a dark path towards some illuminative discovery or revelation or ecstasy, which cannot be willed or obtained through rational knowing.

But again, we would be mistaken if we simply opposed knowing and unknowing – for Keats, negative capability is in some sense "half knowledge," and for apophatic theology unknowing is distinct from *rational* knowledge, but a source of what we might call contemplative "being-with."

Negative theology leads from the sphere of what can be "established" as a being, the sphere where logic is decisive, to a higher sphere where rational language and thought can no longer be regarded as decisive.

(Ernesto Grassi, *Heidegger and the Question of Renaissance Humanism*.)

(For Nicholas of Cusa the transcendent is the limit to what can be known. One *explores* what can be known until one reaches a limit to the reason's means of exploration.)

A *limit*: imageless brilliance, infusing images (and from which all images proceed and return) in the metaphysics of light tradition; imageless darkness (a *dazzling* darkness), in apophatic theology.

((Imagelessness/darkness/the negative –

think of Ad Reinhardt's "black" paintings,

with their

paradoxical coincidence ... of visibility and invisibility, image and imagelessness, form and formlessness, colour and colourlessness, relation and nonrelation, evoking the idea of a transcendent unity.
David Miller, *Art and Disclosure*.))

As a limit to (conceptual) thought: consider also the "Emptiness" of Nāgārjuna's Mahāyāna Buddhist (Madhyamaka) dialectics.

((But we make sense of – we come to see – the way that we ourselves and other beings and things appear in relation to this, through the understanding – through *meanings*.))

IV.

Unknowing: an engagement with the unknown.

>Losing yourself, getting lost –
>>avoiding the paths of knowing, of certitude.

>>>You will find the way to get lost
>>>If you're lucky, blessed.
>>>>(Fanny Howe, "15:18," *O'Clock*.)

A way to get lost. Again, a *dark path*.

In terms of lived possibilities, and our exploration of these possibilities in writing and the other arts, this may involve a sojourning with unease, affliction, even dereliction.

>>(With whatever strips away and unprepares …)

>>Fate eats. God announces itself as affliction, as a pain that is gruesome. God doesn't eat, but wounds. You have to know this in order to live. (Fanny Howe, *Saving History*.)

>>I never met a kinder man than the homeless alcoholic who introduced me to the father of my kids. He was my teacher through a period of my life which was both an actual and an allegorical journey.
>>(…)
>>We had hope. That he would one day be free of his addiction and be able to love someone in health. Now I know we could never love each other more than we did then. Can you understand? Because this is important. We were wrecks, but our relationship was complete. Sufficient. Why ask for more?
>>(…)
>>We were so physically needy that we were freed from our bodies and lived intense spirit-lives. We were the extreme forms that certain human emotions express, but repress too. Extreme affliction frees you, finally, from desire, and so we sought the longest and most difficult

> route to the nirvana of a woodland setting, hand in hand, mind you, and imagining a prospect both physical and internal. A white tree is reflected as a white tree in brown water. No matter what you want to say about it, I saw a pure soul when I saw him.
> (Fanny Howe, *Saving History*.)

To lose oneself – to be moved (shaken –

       thrown) outside of oneself; beyond oneself.

   As in, or by, *compassion*; *mercy*.

> I will tell you how it happened. The hour was the break of dawn and I was lying with a lonely man. We lay on my narrow bed looking out the window onto the sloping slate roofs of a monastery. The damp cheek of the stranger rested by my breast and I felt the sorrow that nursing would very often bring me. I didn't doze but let my sad feelings drift away until the whole of my innerverse had been sucked from my body out the window. While my limbs then lay like wood or paper which had fallen from a great height, my sight looked back. Or of the two souls which occupy the person in a sort of figure eight, the upper one looked back at the lower one. It observed that I was being transported by a quality – magnetic mercy? – which would not be deterred by the white building, or its occupants, or our habits, ethics, acts.
> (Fanny Howe, *The Quietist*.)

This is a movement that is *invisible* or *interior* at the same time as it may issue in visible actions. (And how difficult it is to speak of this movement is reflected in Fanny Howe's recourse to two quite different images – the "innerverse" (innerness) and body, and the two souls "which occupy the person in a sort of figure eight.")

   Another movement that should be mentioned here is that of *turning* –

       turning away,

           turning about,

    turning toward –

to take, decisively, a particular direction – in some way related to *saving, being saved*.

> The air was sweet as lake water. Relaxing wholly, she let herself be carried forward, step by step. Jupiter was the morning star. East by south she walked with the thick sky lifting light from under its rim, as if the sun was its secret and clouds were playing with it.
>
> With no more money and no more alcohol, in a dry state she washed herself in the air, gave herself a new name and aim and disappeared.
> (Fanny Howe, *The Deep North*.)

A writer like Fanny Howe – contemporary American poet and novelist – is aware of just how decisive – literally unto death – this movement may be. Especially in so far as it involves a total commitment to another person – as "Other."

> (The cold water received her weight, but she kept her eyes focused on the boy's face. She really wanted to save his life, seeing him as if he were she – a floating object with one emotion – hope, which made him worthy of the world. And she threw herself at him and hoisted him up, back onto the white shell, where he crawled, like an infant, and called his mother's name in bird-sized peeps, across the crumbling surface.
> (...)
> She floated and dropped, floated and dropped, deeper, in silence and black water, struggled a little, but had to give in, no choice, as if she had performed a task which had taken years of preparation, and which ended in unavoidable rest.
> (Fanny Howe, *In the Middle of Nowhere*.))

((One person is rescued from death; the other, *saved* by a commitment that in this instance leads to death.)))

The actions that result from this inner movement may be seen as *folly*. Again, it is being lost. (Lost to reason and reasonable behavior.) Paul's emphasis on faith in

"Christ crucified"

as

"folly to the Gentiles."

> ... God chose what is foolish in the world to shame the wise, God chose what is weak in the world to shame the strong, God chose what is low and despised in the world, even things that are not, to bring to nothing things that are, so that no human being might boast in the presence of God.
> (*The First Letter of Paul to the Corinthians.*)

(See also the last part of Erasmus' *The Praise of Folly*; as well as John Saward's study, *Perfect Fools: Folly for Christ's Sake in Catholic and Orthodox Spirituality*. Compare, too, the *myōkōnin* or holy fools of Shin Buddhism, together with the central emphasis in Shin on abandoning "self power" for "Other Power.")

Here, too, the notion of believing *because* of the absurdity of belief.

Poverty, too, in the sense of being "poor in spirit." Non-possessiveness; harmlessness. Non-attachment to the world of power, domination, acquisition.

> The face of a human that lives from light, and is open to silence, is usually the face of someone poor. Poverty is not always a condition. It is a way of treating the material world. It is non-dominating. The poor in spirit are those who are – regardless of their condition, up to a point – non-acquisitive, and non-transgressive.
> (Fanny Howe, *Well Over Void.*)

> She felt like a face in an illuminated manuscript, who couldn't get off the beautiful page about G-d.
> (Fanny Howe, *The Lives of a Spirit.*)

(notes)

There are some quotations here and there, but they matter little: or rather, they matter a great deal, but not in terms of naming them. I've always been fond of using other people's words, as it varies the texture of the writing, apart from anything else.

(suddenness)

The poems reflect my involvement with Buddhism (*Jodo Shin-shu*), something in the past and yet also in the present.

David Miller

Notes for *The Dark Path*:

Robin Blaser, 'The Metaphysics of Light', *Capilano Review*, No. 6, North Vancouver, 1974

Boyd & Evans (Fionnuala Boyd and Leslie Evans), from a taped conversation quoted by Bryan Edmondson in the exhibition catalogue *Boyd + Evans 1982-1985*, Wigan: Wigan Education Art Centre, 1985

Jack Chambers, quoted by Nancy Poole, Introduction, *Jack Chambers: Selection of Paintings and Drawings*, London: Canada House Gallery, 1980

Jack Chambers, 'Letter to Simon', *Capilano Review*, No. 33, North Vancouver, 1984

Jaime de Angulo, *Red Indian Tales* (UK edition of *Indian Tales*), London: Heinemann, 1954

Edwin Denby, *Edwin's Tao: Being a Rough Translation of Selections from Lao Tzu's 'Tao Teh Ching'*, NY: Crumbling Empire Press, 1993

Dionysius the Areopagite, *The Mystical Theology and the Celestial Hierarchies*, tr. anonymously, Surrey: The Shrine of Wisdom, 1965

Ernesto Grassi, *Heidegger and the Question of Renaissance Humanism: Four Studies*, Binghampton, NY: SUNY at Binghampton, 1983

Fanny Howe, *The Deep North*, LA: Sun & Moon, 1988

Fanny Howe, *In the Middle of Nowhere*, NY: Fiction Collective, 1984

Fanny Howe, *The Lives of a Spirit*, Sun & Moon, 1987

Fanny Howe, *O'Clock*, London: Reality Street Editions, 1995

Fanny Howe, *The Quietist*, Oakland: O Books, 1992

Fanny Howe, *Saving History*, Sun & Moon, 1993

Fanny Howe, 'Well Over Void', *Five Fingers Review*, #10, San Francisco, 1991

John Keats, *Letters of John Keats: A New Selection*, ed. Robert Gittings, London: OUP, 1970

Joseph Anthony Mazzeo, *Medieval Cultural Tradition in Dante's 'Comedy'*, Ithaca, NY: Cornell University Press, 1960

David Miller, *Art and Disclosure: Seven Essays*, Exeter: Stride Publications, 1998

St. Paul, 'The First Letter of Paul to the Corinthians', *The Holy Bible*, Revised Standard Version, NY: Collins, 1952

Meyer Schapiro, *Words and Pictures: On the Literal and the Symbolic in the Illustration of a Text*, The Hague: Mouton, 1973

Fanny Howe's writings are occasions or loci for a "leap" of insight; sources or supports for spiritual illumination. Like the poems of otherwise dissimilar writers such as Robert Lax, Frank Samperi, or John Riley, they are exemplary in the way they demand that poetry be seen as *spiritual art*. Howe has written:

> "God" scares me, and that's a fact. It also scares me to imagine that I might be seduced by the tones, turns and musics of a poetic tongue which is arranged to create a false idol, an illusion. Babble, excited showing-off, the prettiness of reports coming in from a poetry which is the equivalent of an IQ test. Silence is the only effective and terminal antidote. Before that, it may be the case that the prose line is the least apt to succumb to falsehood. Much of my writing has been an effort to rearrange, rewrite the word "God" by filling up pages with other names. I don't like the name "God" because of its Roman weight. But when I write, I rewrite that name, and then what I write, if it is written well, becomes not a new "God" but a new person, a human face. If a face does not gaze back at me from the page, there is only paper and wood, the static object empty of divine spark. The human face in repose and in silence is the face I see, when what I have written approximates the unspeakable.
>
> (Fanny Howe, *Well Over Void*.)

The Dark Path obviously owes something in terms of its use of format to Mallarmé's *Un coup de dés jamais n'abolira le hasard*, and although I always thought of it as a very unconventional essay, it's not surprising that others have seen it as an essay/poem hybrid.

About the Author

David Miller was born in Melbourne, Australia, but has lived in the UK for many years. His recent publications include *Reassembling Still: Collected Poems* (Shearsman Books, 2014), *Spiritual Letters* (Contraband Books, 2017 / Spuyten Duyvil, 2022), *Towards a Menagerie* (Chax Press, 2019), *Matrix I & II* (Guillemot Press, 2020), *Some Other Days and Nights* (above/ground press, 2021), *Afterword* (Shearsman Books, 2022), *circle square triangle* (Spuyten Duyvil, 2022), *An Envelope for Silence* (above/ground press, 2022), *Some Other Shadows* (Knives Forks and Spoons Press, 2022) and *An Envelope / There and Here* (Spuyten Duyvil, 2022). He is also a painter and a musician.

www.ingramcontent.com/pod-product-compliance
Lightning Source LLC
Chambersburg PA
CBHW051607170426
43196CB00040B/2973